Going Global

Managing the HR Function Across Countries and Cultures

Cat Rickard, Jodi Baker
and Yonca Tiknaz Crew

GOWER

658.3 RIC

Published by
Gower Publishing Limited
Wey Court East
Union Road
Farnham
Surrey GU9 7PT
England

Gower Publishing Company
Suite 420
101 Cherry Street
Burlington, VT 05401-4405
USA

www.gowerpublishing.com

British Library Cataloguing in Publication Data
Rickard, Cat.
  Going global : managing the HR function across countries and cultures. --
  (The Gower HR transformation series)
  1. International business enterprises--Personnel management. 2. Personnel
  management--Cross-cultural studies.
  I. Title II. Series III. Baker, Jodi. IV. Crew, Yonca.
  658.3'009-dc22

  ISBN: 978-0-566-08823-0 (pbk)
  ISBN: 978-0-7546-8134-2 (ebk)

Library of Congress Cataloging-in-Publication Data
Rickard, Cat.
  Going global : managing the HR function across countries and cultures / by
  Cat Rickard, Jodi Baker and Yonca Crew.
    p. cm. -- (The Gower HR transformation series)
  Includes index.
  ISBN 978-0-566-08823-0 (pbk) -- ISBN 978-0-7546-8134-2 (ebook) 1.
  Personnel management. 2. Globalization. I. Baker, Jodi. II. Crew, Yonca.
  III. Title.
  HF5549.R54 2009
  58.3--dc22

                                                              2009011352

Mixed Sources
Product group from well-managed
forests and other controlled sources
www.fsc.org Cert no. SA-COC-1565
FSC © 1996 Forest Stewardship Council

Printed and bound in Great Britain by
MPG Books Group, UK

Contents

List of Figures

List of Tables

PART I
Introduction

① Globalisation and HR

OVERVIEW

A title search on 'globalisation' in the business section of Amazon will typically yield a results list of over 500 books. Refer to the USA Library of Congress Catalogue, and a brief search of books published between 2000 and 2004 will yield a list of more than 5,000 titles published during that period alone. Points of view within these publications vary from 'the world is flat' to 'the world is most definitely still round', and manage to encompass most shapes in between.

Over the last decade countries and their labour markets have made great strides towards global integration. Political and economic reforms have transformed developing countries (such as India, China and those in Eastern Europe) allowing them to compete with the world's superpowers. This ongoing globalisation of the labour market has drawn increasing attention from business commentators, who fall broadly into three groups.

First there are the *sceptics:* those that believe that, if you look back a hundred years, the presence of world trade and mass migration was extremely similar to what it is today. Essentially, *sceptics* ask the question 'what has changed?', and present the argument that where we are today simply represents the logical outcome of a continuum that was in train during the industrial revolution and continued right up to the outbreak of the First World War.

Next there are the *semi-globalisers*: *semi-globalisers* believe that there have been increases in cross-border integration but despite small similarities across borders, they recognise that many huge differences still exist. These differences prevent the development of the genuinely global organisation, and therefore provide real limits on the level of effort organisations should invest in going global.

Lastly there are the *hyper-globalisers*: this group believe that not only are there fundamental changes going on, but that these are so fundamental they have already transformed most of the basic systems and structures of the world. These views tend towards the apocalyptic, based as they are on the concept of complete internationalisation.

Controversial and extreme views grab attention and have always sold well, and a preponderance of literature points towards a relentless march towards a state of inevitable globalisation.

BARRIERS AND ENABLERS TO GLOBALISATION

Were we in a truly 'global' world, you would expect to find no barriers to globalisation, or at least where barriers did exist, a clear set of mitigating actions to overcome them. A brief review of the current situation clearly demonstrates this is not the case.

Significant barriers exist that, while they may not preclude the development of global organisations, certainly put a significant dampener on the process. Although there has been a significant shift in geographic boundaries, in particular since the fall of the Berlin Wall, the nation-state continues to have a pre-eminent position on the global stage, resulting in significant political and administrative barriers to globalisation.

In addition, major obstacles exist in the form of legal barriers, intellectual property regulations and copyrights. The nature of worker protection varies significantly from country to country, and you only need to be asked to manage a European-wide redundancy programme to appreciate the complexities arising in this field alone. The effect of some of the more obvious local differences, including culture and geography, cannot be underestimated, while economic differences may both help and hinder globalisation.

It would be wrong however to jump to the opposite extreme and deny the existence of globalisation altogether. Over the last 20 years a number of enablers have developed to support the delivery of global operations. Technology has enhanced communications, and the growth of telecommunications, the web and effective workflow systems have enabled the delivery of distributed operations. These developments have facilitated the delivery of outsourced and offshored process solutions, further enhancing the geographic base over which solutions can be delivered. Technology changes have also revolutionised the supply chain process, and together with the emergence of new economies, such as China and the Far

East, have encouraged the appearance of new producers and suppliers.

The delivery of operations across a global platform and the servicing of a global market is now feasible. However, this does not mean that organisations are necessarily global in terms of their strategy, structure and intent.

WHERE ARE WE NOW?

At Orion Partners, we believe that economic activity continues to be split between the local and the global stages. The UNATD report now states that there are 63,000 transnational organisations, accounting for 14 per cent of world sales and 12 per cent of employment. There is therefore a mix of organisational focus at play currently, ranging from those with a local, to a regional, and ultimately a global focus. As organisations operate across countries and continents, so too there is an increasing demand for the development of an HR function to support them. This requires the need to rethink the structure of HR, how it is managed and how it operates.

Adopting a fully global model is not the right answer for all organisations. HR has a key role in determining the business strategy in terms of the required scale of operations (that is, local/regional/global), and in delivering the business transformation required to enable this vision once the strategy is agreed. As a result, HR itself must be both able and prepared to transform itself to support the new business model.

This book will provide an outline of the types of activity and capability that are needed to establish an HR function capable of supporting business operations at a regional or global level.

It will focus on two areas, the decision to go global and, once taken, the activities needed to deliver a global HR function. This latter section will focus on three areas: designing the right service; building a cohesive team; and delivering HR talent. It won't address every issue, but will point out some of the key decisions you will need to take, together with advice on your overall approach, and some of the lessons learned by other organisations along the way.

good sentence structure

(2) The Decision to Go Global

To decide whether to go global, you have to answer two key questions. Firstly, does the organisation *want* to go global (and is it ready to do so); and secondly, *what is the best way* to expand operations from a local or regional basis to a global model?

The HR team can provide critical input into both decisions, but is frequently precluded from doing so because organisations tend to adopt a narrow view focused primarily on the financial aspects of strategy. HR is often its own worst enemy when it comes to strategy development, adopting an attitude of simply being an enabling function, rather than being a key stakeholder holding key people-related information that is critical for sound commercial decision making.

ORGANISATIONAL READINESS

Before determining a new business strategy, an organisation must review its readiness to shift to globally-based operations. Organisations that seek to change dramatically the shape of their operations, without adequate planning and reflection, often realise disastrous and unexpected effects on their commercial viability. Delivering clarity of vision, together with a realistic review of readiness, we will touch on all aspects of existing operations and how HR is well placed to facilitate and contribute to this debate.

The change skills of the HR team are critical in helping the organisation develop its vision for the new organisation. What will the new organisation look like? What will the end result look and feel like? How will success be measured? How far along the path to globalisation should the organisation go? Each member of the leadership team may have their own interpretation of the common goal, but it is imperative that they have a consistent and common understanding of the planned outcome, if lack of alignment is not to undermine the transformation from the outset.

Building an aligned leadership team can be achieved through focused discussion aimed at answering a series of structured questions. Key points to consider include:

- What are the benefits of globalisation for our organisation?

- Could these benefits be achieved through pursuit of local or regional strategies?

- What are the issues we face if we do not change?

- Do we intend to globalise through:

  - Adapting to the differences between countries, to become more uniform?
  - Overcoming the differences between countries through standardisation?

- Exploiting the differences between countries to gain competitive advantage?

- What markets do we aim to compete in (local/regional/global)?

- Are we prepared to relinquish our home base?

- What will our future organisation look and feel like?

- What are the barriers and enablers to the transition (internal and external)? → *How is the environment?*

- How will we measure success?

The level of organisational inclusion in the debate will vary from organisation to organisation. The results of these discussions will form the basis for the new business strategy, and must be summarised formally in a clearly articulated way, that will be understood by staff across all territories and business units.

ORGANISATIONAL TRANSFORMATION

Having established the imperative and vision for the organisational transformation, you need to take strategic decisions on the method that will be used to achieve your vision.

Although the current economic turmoil of 2008/09 has temporarily damped down activity, globalisation has exponentially increased the market for cross border mergers and acquisitions, offshoring deals and joint ventures. In 1996 alone, there were over 2,000 cross border transactions, worth close to $300 billion. Strategies for expansion included:

- Cost savings through consolidation, with the elimination of duplication and economies of scale often achieved through acquisitions.

- Revenue enhancement through the merging of complimentary strengths and capabilities.

- Process improvement through the transfer of non core competencies to specialist providers via global sourcing.

- Achievement of tax benefits through tax structuring and tax planning via joint ventures.

The execution of such strategies without the involvement of HR is perilous. In these circumstances, the case for the organisation to go global is based on the hard benefits of entering into new market territory, buying out competitors, and transferring the management of processes to others who will perform them better and cheaper. However, the achievement of these benefits is predicated on the contribution of HR to the transition plan.

In many cases, the HR due diligence on such transactions focuses simply on the financial aspects associated with, for example, executive remuneration, terms and conditions, and the likely pensions liability involved. This input is driven by the business case that underpins the transaction, which may focus only on the financial aspects of the transaction, to the exclusion of key considerations such as people, culture and styles of working, all of which define the long-term success of a global organisation.

Ignoring these human elements is dangerous. If overlooked, the strategy for global expansion may appear worthwhile on paper, but could turn out to be disappointing. A 1999 KPMG study highlighted that when only examining the hard facts (financial matters) in the case of mergers and acquisitions, one half to one third of organisations seeking global status didn't live up to their potential, up to 83 per cent didn't add value and even more worryingly, 53 per cent destroyed value.

Some of the highest profile examples are the AOL-Time Warner deal which lost 93 per cent of its value during the integration period and VeriSign which, while acquiring Network Solutions, lost $17 billion and experienced a 98 per cent fall in the value of their stock; all further evidence of the key role of HR in the process of going global.

THE CONTRIBUTION OF HR TO REALISING THE ORGANISATION'S VISION

Strong HR leadership should be at the forefront of the transformation. An important consideration for the CEO is the skillset required of the HRD and HR team to drive the process.

For example, within the food industry where a policy of acquisition and aggressive cost cutting is adopted, the retention of key individuals within the acquisition will be critical, while the loss of a large portion of the workforce (for example, the management layers to team leader level) will be highly desirable. The HR department in this instance would need to be well versed in restructuring, downsizing and headcount reduction.

This is in stark contrast to a merger of two professional services organisations, which requires an HR department with significant skills in organisation development, talent retention and cultural integration, if the workforce (and importantly the associated client base) is to be retained. In such circumstances, the HR department will need to initiate work during the due diligence stage to assess the culture of the potential target. Figure 2.1 illustrates the varying types of people strategies that could be adopted depending on the desired outcome of the merger.

An appropriate human resources strategy should drive an entire integration plan, including change, communication, process and policy change, and the HR activities needed to complete the transition.

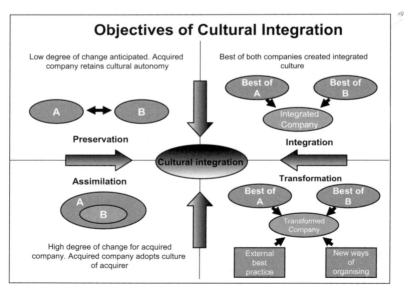

Figure 2.1   Objectives of cultural integration

The situation is similar for an organisation evaluating their global sourcing options. Again, HR has a key role to play, for example in determining if this effort to globalise ways of working would prove acceptable to its employees. HR must recognise that in a paternalistic culture, global sourcing would most likely be perceived negatively. You need to understand and communicate the fact that the evident culture clash between the global strategy and the organisation's rooted culture could potentially negate the intended benefits.

Once an outsourcing decision is taken, HR has a role in deciding which activities could be offshored or outsourced. The selection of activities for outsourcing essentially underpins decisions made regarding where to locate these activities and identifies which provider is best fit to deliver them. For example, in outsourcing sales, order capture and processing, the culture and brand of the organisation must be replicated by the outsource provider within the service centre, if the expectations of customers are to be met. Only the HR team will be in a position to identify and measure the underlying values and behaviours that must be replicated within the service centre, if the end-to-end processes are to be delivered seamlessly from the customers' perspective.

Setting up a joint venture to achieve global status is another operation requiring the input of the HR team. In those circumstances, HR needs to provide help and guidance on how best to manage their subsidiaries and partnering organisations but they also need to overcome legal issues in setting up operations worldwide. Furthermore, they must seek to outline and define Service Level Agreements (SLAs) between their organisation and the joint venture, and seek to measure this effectively with an output of accurate management information.

THE CONTRIBUTION OF HR TO SUSTAINING THE ORGANISATION'S VISION

It is likely that in any shift towards global operations, some significant changes will be required in the way the organisation is structured, operates and behaves. The nature and priority of these changes will be determined by the precise make-up of the strategy adopted by the organisation. The HR strategy that will enable delivery of the business strategy must be clearly defined before work can commence on any specific interventions. However, it is probable that the contribution of HR will be integral in a number of areas:

- Recruitment – At its most basic level, HR may be required to staff up new territories and markets rapidly in support of organisational expansion. New alternatives may need to be sought as high quality staff become a scarce commodity in emerging markets. For example, some organisations are now establishing call centres to service Japan on the east coast of China, where there is a ready supply of cheap resource with the appropriate language skills to service this market.

- At a more complex level, although significant change can be delivered through effective learning and development interventions, often the fastest way to engender a shift in the workforce is through changes to the recruitment process and policy. For example, staff may be required to operate in new environments and contexts, and with a wider diversity of colleagues. It may be simplest to start recruiting people who are disposed to working in such situations.

- Talent development – Many organisations now provide specialist courses in other countries, offering employees language and cross-cultural training, before undertaking a short sabbatical of up to a year in the relevant country. The provision of expatriate assignments for key talent also represents a good way to foster cross-regional and global linkages.

- Establishing core values – Organisations, for example professional services firms, deliberately develop a strong culture and set of core values to build a 'one firm' approach. This can be a good way of overcoming the risk of parochialism, without overriding the strong contribution that local and regional variations make to the organisation as a whole.

- Fostering cross-border activity – HR can perform a key role in maintaining an organisation-wide view of skills and capabilities, and channelling this information to support participation in regional and global teams and projects. The delivery of key conferences from different locations, and the geographical dispersion of business unit HQs and Centres of Excellence also provides a strong visible indicator of the organisation's priorities and strategy.

- Development – The HR teams of most global organisations now deliver a significant portion of their learning and development activities through some form of regional or global academy or university. Activities, whether involving classroom interaction or other media, provide a strong cohesive influence, and again the balance between locally, regionally and globally designed and delivered interventions is very important.

It is also imperative that the HR team clearly understand the measures they will use to assess the success of the specific interventions, as well as the HR strategy overall, before embarking on the delivery.

SUMMARY

The contribution of HR to the development of a global strategy includes a number of key contributions and outcomes:

- Driving the leadership team to build a clearly articulated vision for the future organisation (whether it be local, regional or global in base).

- Aligning the leadership to this vision.

- Reviewing the readiness of the organisation to change, including an assessment of both internal and external barriers and enablers.

- Helping determine the approach to delivering the global organisation.

- Supporting the transition.

- Helping to sustain the new organisation.

The remainder of this book will focus on the core challenge for HR itself; how to transform itself to enable delivery of the business strategy and the new organisation.

PART II

Delivering
a Global HR
Function

③ Getting the Strategy Right

Once the organisation's overall vision and strategy is defined, each function will then develop their own strategy and plan to enable the delivery of the whole. The challenge for HR in doing so is two-fold:

- Firstly, it must have a sufficient understanding of both the organisational vision, and the component function/business unit strategies that will deliver against this if it is to understand the service it will need to deliver to the organisation.

- Secondly, it must define its own strategy and vision that underpins how it will deliver this service.

There may be a risk of a significant gap between strategy development, and the implementation of the strategy itself. It is important to bridge this gap by ensuring the vision for the new service is clear, and the principles against which the service will be designed and delivered are identified and supported, both by HR and the business.

In defining the service design principles, it is important to canvass opinion through use of structured interviews, and to define the desired business outcome based on those principles.

Figure 3.1 provides an example of the type of outcome-driven service design principles that can be used to ensure the service is in line with the business strategy.

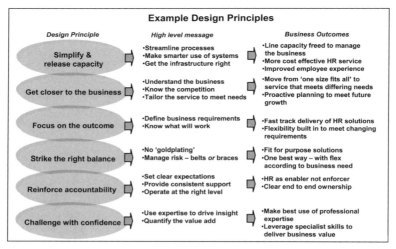

Figure 3.1   Example design principles

In developing the design principles, remember to consider the wider range of principles that will be used to guide the design across the full range of HR components.

For example, in defining these principles, it is important to determine the balance between local and global activities (see Figure 3.2) if the principles are to be clear, unambiguous and easy to use. The principles defined above represent those of a global bank, which for the first time was seeking to deliver significant standardisation across the HR function, through the implementation of a new software platform and the implementation of the Ulrich model (Ulrich, 1997).

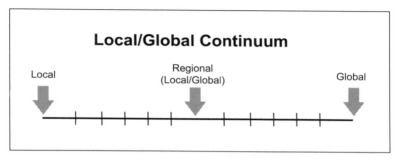

Figure 3.2   The local/global continuum

In this instance, the bank aimed to deliver a globally consistent service, which deviated only where local circumstances (legal or business case related) dictated. For other organisations, a position closer towards the 'Local' end of the continuum may be more appropriate. Using the Local/Global Continuum model is a useful way to determine what level of globalisation is actually required, and the business outcomes that will be driven as a result.

This model can be applied across a number of HR components, as appropriate, to inform the decision-making process. There is no right or wrong answer here: positive business outcomes may be achieved at either end of the continuum. The key outcome is the quality of the debate, and the right balance between local and global focus for your organisation to deliver the required business outcomes. An example is provided overleaf (Table 3.1).

Table 3.1   HR components on the local/global continuum

No	Aspect	Local	Regional	Global
1	HR Process	Each country has different processes – differences driven by legal, local policy and system variations	Processes are consistent across regions OR mix of local with some regional consistency	Single global process with local variations only where driven by legal barriers/ business case
	HR Implication	Significant retraining required if HR staff move across boundaries	Opportunities for deployment of HR staff with some retraining required	HR staff can be deployed globally with minimal retraining required
	Business Outcome	Internationally mobile employees will experience a significant variation in HR service	Internationally mobile employees will experience some variation in HR service	HR service should largely be consistent across all countries
2	HR Policy	Policies vary from country to country	Some standardisation of key policies	Single global policy exists for large proportion of HR policies
	HR Implication	Centres of excellence have to cater for significant policy variation	Regional centres of excellence can accommodate some local variation	Global centres of excellence with pools of local expertise where required are feasible
	Business Outcome	Excessive variation/ complexity hinders business flexibility	Balance between consistent and locally driven policy	Too rigid policy/excessive standardisation hinders flexibility in working within new markets

Table 3.1   *Concluded*

No	Aspect	Local	Regional	Global
3	HR Systems	High level of local variation	Some consistency across regions, for example, manual intervention to generate cross-regional HRMI	Single platform and application with minimal variation (for example, payroll only) allows global processes
	HR Implication	Significant effort required to generate regional/global HRMI	Some manual effort required to consolidate global MI	Capacity to focus on analysis of automatically produced HRMI
	Business Outcome	HR value added activities are at a minimum	HR teams have some capacity to focus on partnering the business	Full business partnering model is feasible
4	HR Components	No standard components, for example, T&Cs vary country to country	T&Cs vary across regions but some cross regional components exist, for example, standard grades for senior management	Single approach to grading structure
	HR Implication	Organisation design focus is at a local level	Development of some consistency in regional structures is possible	Development of global teams and structures is feasible
	Business Outcome	Team structures are focused at a local level	Team structures can be adapted at a regional level to attain consistency	Development of global specialist teams is supported

Once the exact location of the various components that make up the HR function has been determined on the Local/Global Continuum, the development of the new HR function itself can begin. There are three key areas that must be addressed if an effective HR function is to be delivered.

HR must:

- Design the service to deliver the required business outcomes (whether this entails managing all processes centrally or encompassing a hybrid approach to managing some processes globally and others regionally or locally to meet specific needs).

- Build a cohesive team to deliver the service (whether the model developed is a single shared service centre, or a set of regionally based hubs delivering subtly different services to meet local requirements).

- Deliver HR talent – that is, highly capable individuals in the key roles (whether this talent is generated from a single global pool, or from multiple regional/local talent pools).

The following chapters of this book consider each of these challenges in turn, and what activities must be undertaken if a global HR function is to be delivered.

(4) Designing the Right Service

Delivering a new HR function capable of operating effectively on a global stage represents a significant challenge, not only in terms of the investment required to deliver the new function, but also in terms of the level of sponsorship and collaboration required to take and drive through some of the difficult decisions that will be encountered along the way.

Designing a global function is not as straightforward as simply scaling up existing local structures and activities. Work will include:

- Recognising and working with the barriers to global operations.

- Identifying new processes needed to operate at a global level.

- Deciding which processes must reside at a global level, and which can continue with local or regional variation.

- Acquiring the right tools and technology to support the service.

- Realigning the structure of HR to deliver the new service.

- Identifying new skills and capabilities needed to deliver the new function.

- Managing the expectations of the business.

STARTING OFF ON THE RIGHT FOOT

As with any organisational change, it is critical to ensure that the design of the function is robust and will deliver the service required by the business.

Only with the right resources, sponsorship and governance in place will an appropriate design be delivered. All too often, HR teams fail to commit to the transformation, and as a result fail to deliver a function capable of delivering against the business strategy. This issue is exacerbated when attempting to work at a global level. Many organisations have HR leaders for each business unit, or by geography, with inadequate or no overall leadership capable of driving forward the required level of integrated activity.

The level of sponsorship and internal commitment required to deliver this degree of change is significant. A robust business case, detailing both quantified and non-quantified benefits, is vital to the success of the transformation. This is of particular importance where enabling technology is required to deliver the transformation, or where it is anticipated that significant costs will be incurred through the reduction of the existing

HR team or recruitment of new resources. The business case should detail benefits from both an HR and a business perspective. It should accompany a clearly articulated case for change, detailing why the transformation is needed and the likely outcomes for both HR and the business if no action is taken.

Both the business case and the case for change should be signed off by HR and business leaders, and a clear governance model for the transformation should be established. The model will contain both clearly identified sponsors, representing the different areas of HR (be they business unit or geography related), and a clearly defined path for issues escalation and resolution.

In addition, the scope of the transformation needs to be clearly defined (for example, detailing if there are any exclusions, or any areas which are outside the remit of the transformation). Delivering change on a global scale makes it doubly important that good practice project management processes and structures are put in place, and a rigorous project initiation document or charter should be developed outlining the who, what, when, where and how of the transformation.

RECOGNISING CONSTRAINTS

As has already been noted, moving to a global model does not necessarily mean that every aspect of HR delivery has to be globalised. A key decision to be made early on is the level to which process and organisation standardisation should and will be driven through the design.

A number of good reasons exist as to why certain processes and structures may continue to exist at a local rather than a global level. These include:

- Variations in the expectations of the workforce. For example, in certain cultures, self-service may be considered to be the most effective and satisfactory way of updating employee details. In other cultures, self-service may be unacceptable, and there may be a clear expectation that a simple phone call should enable the changes to be completed. These variations are not necessarily driven by the culture associated with different countries and regions. Different business units within a global organisation may have very different views on what is an appropriate and an inappropriate activity for them to complete.

  For example, in law firms, self-service is rarely completed by partners. This type of activity is deemed too clerical and is delegated to secretarial staff. Similarly, in banks, wholesale teams, in particular traders, are often considered too valuable a commodity to spend time in basic administrative activities, and variations may be required.

  Within a fully developed shared service model, it is possible to accommodate such variations in service through the design of different charging levels, according to the level of support required. Where a full model is not developed, for example as a result of the relatively immature level of HR, or as a result of taxation issues associated with such models when applied on a global basis, then it may be necessary to cater for such local variations.

- Variations in legal requirements across different geographies. For example, the implementation of systems involving global databases is often complicated by data protection issues. This can be problematic, for example when seeking to share data between Europe and the USA, where very different data protection laws exist.

Other variations exist in the level of worker protection. In particular, employment legislation and regulations in place across Europe vary widely, with very different arrangements covering the representation of employees' rights, for example through Trade Unions or Works Councils. Regulations vary widely when it comes to the question of terminations, consultation and notification periods, as well as the level of severance payments that is required across different geographies.

- Variations in economic conditions. Again, very different circumstances exist across a global stage. In developed countries, reward and remuneration packages may be complex and sophisticated, including for example, performance-related pay and bonus calculations. Flexible benefits packages may exist, together with employee pension schemes involving varying degrees of employer contribution. Complex benefit in kind arrangements may also be in place, for example access to a staff shop, discount schemes or communal dinning facilities. In poorer economies, it is likely that remuneration is simpler, and focused on a basic pay and bonus structure.

Variations in reward and remuneration may arise as a result of a history of mergers and acquisitions. Where such transactions occur without an attempt to standardise benefits and terms and conditions, a complex array of reward and remuneration policies and practices may exist within the same geography or business unit.

- Variations in language and culture. Although it is the most obvious constraint, the impact of language and cultural differences in developing a global HR function should not be underestimated. The outsourcing of call centres to India during the late 20th Century, where a cheap, educated resource with the right language skills was available to deliver customer services, became a commonplace activity. So commonplace, in fact, that many organisations within the UK are now differentiating themselves by marketing the fact that they run their call centres from within the UK.

As different economies emerge, different geographic opportunities arise to source the type of resource needed to deliver shared service functions. For example, Slovakia is becoming an increasingly popular location for shared service centre set-up, overtaking Poland which was previously the first choice for northern European shared service and call centre start-ups.

Allied to this is the need to consider different time zones. Many organisations are demanding HR services that will deliver 24/7, even though the cost analysis for such service is often dubious. It is however an important consideration when shifting to a global model.

The key question in determining the level of standardisation required is whether or not any business benefit will be delivered as a result of the transformation, whether the business requires this level of standardisation and whether this balances out against the issues and constraints that must be addressed in delivering this type of service.

(5) Focusing on the Right Processes

The identification of new global processes (such as expatriate movement, or multi-currency remuneration), together with the need to retain a degree of local processing as a result of country specific requirements, results in a HR service which is a blend of local, regional and global elements.

An important first step is to identify which processes will be standardised globally, and which will continue to vary by location.

Typically, the processes which are of the most strategic value are the ones that HR will focus on standardising globally. Table 5.1 shows the different approach taken by five different organisations to this issue, and the very different solutions that were adopted to meet business needs. The processes highlighted with an X in each column indicate processes that were standardised.

The decision as to which processes to standardise globally will vary according to the service requirements of your organisation, and the business strategy to be enabled. It is useful to clarify

Table 5.1   Example global processes

Standardised Process	Company 1	Company 2	Company 3	Company 4	Company 5
Benefits	x	x	x	x	
Compensation	x	x	x		x
Recruitment	x	x	x	x	x
Development	x		x	x	x
Diversity		x		x	x
Measurement/ metrics	x			x	
Information system	x		x	x	x
Operations			x	x	
General queries	x				
Tools	x		x		x

business requirements before embarking on what will likely be a complex and difficult transformation. Structured interviews with key business stakeholders can provide a useful input, and together with other diagnostic information can form a sound basis for the prioritisation of work. Sample diagnostic questions include:

- What is the cost of the process (for example, HR cost per Full Time Employee- FTE)?

- How important is the effectiveness of this process (what are the performance and effectiveness metrics)?

- How important is this process to the employee (for example, survey data from business users)?

- How important is consistency in the delivery of this process?

- How important is efficiency in the delivery of this process?

- How important is quality in the delivery of this process?

As a general rule, there are a number of important reasons why organisations may choose to develop global processes for specific activities. Table 5.2 provides a sample of some of the key reasons for process globalisation.

Table 5.2   Reasons for process globalisation

HR Process	Reason for Process Globalisation
Employee data management for a number of core items	For global reporting and tracking employee data
Compensation	Consistent approach to reward, disseminating a united feel while easing the use of relocation
Workforce planning and reporting	Enabling central information which can be used to identify and create solutions for over and underperforming locations
Performance management	To have consistent measures of performance and for the perceptions of fairness
Resourcing for certain roles	Making sure that people with sufficient capabilities are in charge of global process
360° reviews	To have a consistent feedback system globally
Talent management	To have a connected talent strategy where employees can be tracked and developed globally
Relocation and expatriates	Consistency of approach. Important in developing talent and disseminating knowledge across locations
HRIS support	To maximise the consistency in data management

The desire to standardise globally has to be balanced by the different type of local variations that exist. For example, for a company operating in multiple locations, the employee relations service that is required for the USA and Germany will vary as a result of the differences in unionisation and work council involvements. This may lead to the process being defined locally in Germany, because staff operating there need to have the right skills and specialisms to engage with work councils. Sharing a common process with the USA would not represent a viable option.

However, there may be sufficient similarities in worker protection across European countries that a regional process for employee relations could be set up. This would deliver tailored proficiency in local legal, commercial, government and cultural issues as well as language proficiency when required.

Organisations should seek to manage some processes in-country, in particular where fiscal and legislative differences are of significance. Table 5.3 provides a sample of some of the key reasons for process localisation.

The right balance of global and local processes can be achieved in 3 different ways:

1. Clearly defining which processes are global and which will be regional/local, for example, Management Development will be delivered globally, while Payroll will be delivered locally.

2. Defining within process areas what will be driven globally and what will be delivered regionally/locally, for example, Talent Management for the top three structural levels of

the organisation will be completed globally, for the next two structural levels will be completed regionally, and for remaining structural levels will be completed locally.

3. Defining a global process template, but allowing a percentage variation for regional and local implementation, for example, all activities within a defined scope will be delivered through global processes. However, in implementation, up to 20 per cent of the standard process may be varied to fit the local context.

The likely outcome of this piece of work will be a hybrid solution, consisting of a mix of global, regional and locally driven processes.

Table 5.3   Reasons for process localisation

HR Process	Reasons for Process Localisation
Payroll, time and attendance	Differences in taxation and working hours
Leave administration	Local differences in leave arrangements and expectations
Local recruitment and staffing	For attracting local talent and recruiting most effectively with suitable tools
Benefits administration	Variations in approach as a result of local economic conditions and expectations
Pensions	Variations in country practice and legislation
Local delivery of training courses/programmes etc	To design programs which are suitable to local learning culture
Employment relation resolution and case work	To accommodate differences in employment legislation and grievance/disciplinary practices

(6) Acquiring the Right Tools

Having defined the scope of process change required, it is likely that a significant investment will be required to upgrade existing software and IT systems to provide a consistent platform from which to deliver the global processes.

The key challenge facing organisations shifting to a global operational focus is to consolidate data into a single format and data store, enabling the delivery of 'one version of the truth' with minimal need for the manual manipulation or double handling of data. This change is often complicated by the existence of an array of legacy systems, which store subtly different data items, making the generation of basic comparable MI difficult. In other instances, a single software application may exist, but one that has been implemented using a different data model across different regions, creating a different set of challenges for the HR project team responsible for driving process consistency.

Even where minimal system renewal is required, significant effort may be needed to complete data cleansing activities, to ensure the basic information captured is correct. All too often, organisations are unable to pinpoint accurately even basic information, such as how many HR staff they have, as a result of the creation of non-standard system role types and the misfiling of staff into the wrong categories.

Completing software selection on a global basis is an exponentially more complex activity than at a local level, as a result both of the increased number of requirements, and the number of internal stakeholders that have to be engaged and included in the process and decision making. In addition, it can be extremely expensive, with the spectre of ongoing implementation costs as software applications have to be maintained to the latest version.

An alternative approach to reducing costs whilst improving operations, efficiency and quality is to embark on a global outsourcing deal. Outsourcing enables organisations to:

- Keep core strategic activities in-house, whilst moving out non value-add processes.

- Focus the HR team on value-add processes, whilst outsourcing administrative activities.

- Enable greater cost management, performance tracking and accountability.

Different types of outsourcing deals are available, from ones where the vendor runs your IT systems for you, to ones where the vendor completes the transformation and runs your processes using their own software systems and staff. This has the advantage of removing the need for sourcing expensive global IT solutions, together with the associated implementation costs. Processes may be outsourced to a single or to multiple vendors, for example, payroll and pensions provision may be divided across two different specialist vendors. Some of the key drivers for outsourcing include the need to:

- Improve organisational performance.

- Focus on core competencies.

- Align HR closer with the strategic people-related aspects of business processes by reducing administrative duties.

- Reduce and control operating costs by:

    - Eliminating duplication of efforts, especially in a decentralised or geographically dispersed company.
    - Eliminating the cost of acquiring, updating and maintaining systems in-house.
    - Transitioning processes to organisations who are able to attain products and services at less cost due to specific know-how and scale economies.

- Improve process efficiency and effectiveness and increase customer service.

- Eliminate difficult-to-manage functions.

- Improve reliability and consistency of HR products and services.

- Gain access to the expertise of specialists who offer best-practice advice and help improve service to employees.

- Obtain access to world-class technology and other resources.

Again, you need to select with care which processes will be outsourced and which will be retained. This decision is driven by determining which processes are low value and administrative in nature, and which represent a significant value-added activity for the organisation. The diagram below (Figure 6.1) provides an example of some of the processes most frequently targeted for outsourcing by organisations.

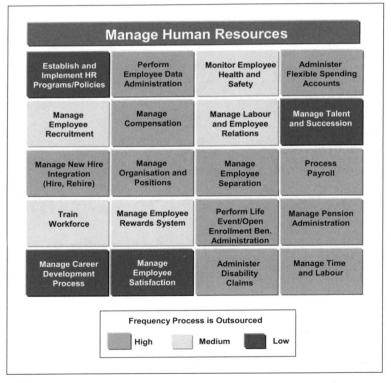

Figure 6.1   Frequency processes are outsourced

Processes may be further prioritised, to gain a comprehensive picture of what should be outsourced, and how quickly. The following categories can be used to evaluate priority:

- Urgency of issue.

- Timeline of implementation.

- Fit with HR goals and objectives.

- Probability of success.

- Cost savings – quick hits, short-term and long-term.

- Service improvements.

It is not necessary to limit the focus of outsourcing to basic administrative processes. In deciding what to 'make and buy', it is critical that the organisation carefully considers which processes represent the delivery of real strategic value, that is, which activities represent a core organisational competence. It would be all to easy for example, to consider which aspects of the Ulrich HR delivery model[1] should be outsourced, and limit these areas to basic HR administration, or focus solely on activities completed within the Shared Service Centre.

In fact, there may be services across every building block of the model which could be considered as target areas for outsourcing. Figure 6.2 provides examples of the types of activity that may be outsourced, including, in more progressive

1   Ulrich, D. (1997) *Human Resources Champions: The Next Agenda for Adding Value and Delivery Results*, Harvard Business School Press.

outsourcing arrangements, aspects of the Business Partnering role itself.

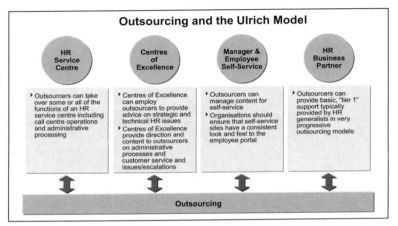

Figure 6.2   Outsourcing and the Ulrich Model

Before taking any final decisions regarding whether to outsource, a number of key considerations should be taken into account:

- Level of business-specific knowledge required to effectively deliver the process/function and whether an outsource provider vendor can achieve this level of knowledge.

- Overall business risk associated with the potential alternative.

- Implementation approach and timing.

- Opportunity to realise up front and long-term return on investment.

- Feasibility of acquiring deep expertise and the skill sets required to implement and maintain the selected sourcing solution (HR, technology, service centre and so on).

- Alignment to IT strategy and direction.

- Ease of delivery model to support future acquisitions and divestitures.

- Requirements for customer support for all locations (that is, 'follow the sun' support, regional service centres, multi-language and culture support, global data networks and so on).

Evaluation of the vendors should not focus solely on price and contractual terms. It is important to consider their reputation, track record, existing customer base, and existing relationships. Cultural fit will be important, as will their potential to provide additional value-added capability.

Again, as in the case of IT vendor evaluation and selection, completing a global outsourcing deal will be significantly more complex than a simple local arrangement, as a result both of the increased number of requirements and the number of internal stakeholders that have to be engaged and included in the process and decision making. The list below provides some of the key lessons learned by organisations that have embarked on global sourcing solutions.

Lessons learnt:

- Sourcing decisions that are strictly cost driven are more at risk of failure.

- Organisational culture and the operating environment within HR are the greatest determinants of success of which sourcing solutions will and will not work.

- The ROI on sourcing investments will not be realised unless the service delivery model and the scope of services are clearly defined up front.

- HR change management (that is, redesigning the organisation and business processes to fit the new solution) is vital to ensure ROI.

- Sourcing solutions most often result in new capability requirements:

  - *Insourcing*: Enhancements to the operational infrastructure (processes, technology, knowledge and skill requirements).
  - *Outsourcing*: Establishment of an effective vendor management methodology (performance standards, measurement mechanisms and so on).
  - *Co-sourcing*: Operational infrastructure enhancements and effective vendor management methodology.

(7) Focusing on the Right Structures

A core component of any service delivery model is the underlying structure that will be put in place to deliver the new processes (where not outsourced). Just as organisations may choose to adopt a phased approach to delivering standard processes using a standard system and database, so the shift to one organisation per process via one location can be undertaken gradually.

For example, where adopting the Ulrich model (or near equivalent), it may be desirable to phase the transition, shifting from country-based support, to regional, to global or even a virtually-based HR model. Organisations can be reluctant to inflict this level of change on their business users. However, with careful planning this type of transition can be delivered almost seamlessly. For example, in the case of a global hardware provider, the organisation went through three delivery phases, which were largely transparent to end users.

During the first phase, a single point of contact was established for staff along with a help desk for managers. This channel routed employees through to the relevant country-based case management team, who had recourse to a nascent regional specialist team for the escalation of difficult cases. In the second phase, both staff and managers were routed through a single point of contact, while the country-based case teams began to rationalise into regional teams. During the final phase, the structure became almost a mirror image of the Phase One structure, with all queries routed through to regional case management teams, who could call on country specialists for local expert input as required.

In terms of how a country/regional/global split is achieved, the exact solution depends on the nature of the service required by the specific organisation. Nor is it critical to deliver the entire Ulrich structure – many organisations choose to implement only the Shared Service Centre (SSC), or SSC and Business Partner components. However, where the full model is implemented, a number of common themes do emerge:

- The HR Leadership Team is typically based globally, with the Group Head of HR or equivalent generally based out of the HQ (where still in place). Frequently, designated global process owners are identified to lead on specific areas, for example, strategy, policy, ongoing process integrity, but not for operational activities.

- The Business Partner team is usually aligned by Business Unit or Division, subdivided by regions, areas and potentially by country. The team is scaled to provide some form of 'face-to-face' support for a pre-defined management group. Although this can lead to significant issues when organisations decide to restructure, this remains the dominant model.

- Centres of Excellence (CoE) are often affected by outsourcing, with outsourced areas treated as a CoE in their own right. Areas that remain in-house tend to either be based within specific geographic locations, or operate virtually. In some instances, where the teams operate virtually, the teams are even located with the local Business Partner teams and are aligned to the business. The important thing is they reflect the size and location of the population that represents their primary customer.

  The subject specialisms of the CoE vary from organisation to organisation; an example from the finance sector included: resourcing and executive development, reward and recognition, education and learning, organisation development, and individual executive development, all of which were identified as the core areas for that organisation. Typically there is a global head of CoE, with segment or process owner leads reporting in per subject area.

- Shared services are most frequently delivered using two or more service centres. Although to end users the service may appear global, in fact when it comes to delivery, operations remain on a regional level. In latter years, Canada, the UK and India have been popular locations, although increasingly other areas are becoming predominant, for example Slovakia within Europe. Very often, the 'home' location for an organisation becomes the location of one of the regional SSC hubs.

  For example, in the case of a global car manufacturer, three locations were selected in the shortlist for location, in North America, Sweden, and France (see Figure 7.1).

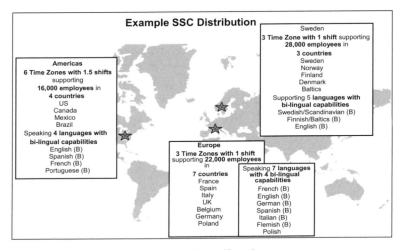

Figure 7.1   Example SSC distribution

- In designing the SSC, many organisations find it preferable to over-resource initially and reduce headcount post-implementation, as under-resourcing has the tendency to undermine the integrity and effectiveness of the overall model

Once again, the structure selected and the balance between local and global roles is dependent on the type and quality of HR service an organisation requires. In most implementations, organisations cite the absolute criticality of engaging stakeholders throughout the process and in particular during the design phase, to ensure HR, business and employee buy-in.

There are four key factors for consideration when creating an effective global HR service (see Figure 7.2).

Figure 7.2   **Factors for consideration in creating an effective global HR service**

These include:

- Levels and type of HR interaction with employees.

- Types of service to be delivered – time, quality and cost.

- Varying degrees of support required by different business units/end users.

- The adoption of differences in knowledge and experience.

The decision on the type of structure to adopt will vary according to the response to these questions. Designing the delivery model must include consultation with business and HR teams (under appropriate non-disclosure arrangements) and the involvement of key stakeholders in decision making. These stakeholders should:

- Represent a variety of structural levels within the organisation.

- Include a mix of business and HR staff.

- Represent the different business units.

- Represent the key geographies involved.

You can involve stakeholders through the use of surveys, facilitated group sessions or interviews, allowing a variety of opinions on HR's structure to be gained, validated and consolidated. The questions posed should seek to tease out what type of service is expected from HR and how the function should be both deployed and organized. The initial results, based on the information gathered concerning the desired structure, should then be validated with the same groups.

Canvassing the opinion of employees and managers can often lead to an overly negative view of the transition. For example, line managers may complain bitterly about their HR managers (HRMs) and the quality of service they receive, until it is suggested those HRMs might be taken away from them. Information gathered from the business therefore needs to be carefully analysed, and a reality check taken. Table 7.1 provides examples of typical questions to ask your stakeholders, as well as specific questions for HR to consider based upon their responses.

Table 7.1   Typical stakeholder questions

	STAKEHOLDER QUESTIONS	HR QUESTIONS
1.	Are you comfortable with ringing someone for policy advice instead of accessing a face-to-face service?	Is this response unique to this location?
2.	Is there a difference if you access a service from someone 100km away or someone 500km away?	Is this response a preference or a reality?
3.	Do you feel comfortable seeking advice from someone on a different continent?	Is this response based on habit?
4.	On average how often do you require high-priority people or policy advice?	What is the variation in demands in terms of size between business units?
5.	Do you understand the difference between administrative and strategic queries?	Do they understand how to use their HR service?

Regardless of the solution selected, it is very important to ensure a representative group of senior sponsors are engaged in the review and sign-off of the final design. This will become particularly significant as the go live date of the transition to the new service approaches.

More often than not, a measurable proportion of management will be reluctant to move to the new model, partly as a result of the loss of their personal HR resources (in the form of the HRMs), and partly as a result of the introduction of self-service, which is often perceived as a shift in workload from HR to the line. Significant effort should be invested in getting the change management, communication and training activities right prior to the launch of the new service, to ensure expectations are appropriately managed, and the transition to the new service is as smooth as possible.

MANAGING EXPECTATIONS

Achieving the right balance in managing line expectations for the new service can be difficult. Often for the bulk of line management and staff, changes to the HR function are perceived as ancilliary to their 'day job', and are of limited interest. Being at the receiving end of an overly heavy change plan can be extremely aggravating to line users, who may have the attitude 'tell me what I need to do differently when I need to do it differently, and not before'. It is critical therefore to build a sound understanding of the level of change readiness of the organisation, and in particular the scale of change activities appropriate for the business.

Clear, timely and appropriate communication about the changes in the HR service is the key. The business can only use HR properly when they have the right information regarding what they need to complete, and what HR will deliver for them in return.

There are a number of deliverables that need to be completed to ensure the design is robust, and the most important service changes are flagged effectively to the business, to HR and to the support teams. Figure 7.3 shows the hierarchy of materials you need to produce.

Core to the design are the service specifications and role profiles, which define who does what. These details can then be:

- Summarised to produce Line Manager and Employee Guides.

- Broken into further detail to produce:

- Job descriptions and process maps, that will define how the service will be delivered.
- Work instructions and training guides, that will ensure HR teams understand how to deliver the new service.

Two tools are of particular use in delivering Line Manager and Employee Guides.

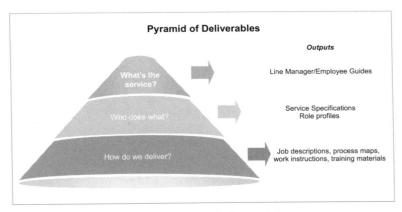

Figure 7.3   The pyramid of deliverables

START-STOP-CONTINUE GUIDES

Start-stop-continue guides (Figure 7.4) are materials that HR can create to allow their customers to understand what they must do to access HR's new service, and what they should expect to receive and not receive as part of that service.

The stop-start-continue guide is a light touch form of training material. It should clearly communicate the key changes and describe in sufficient detail what the employees need to do differently in the new world. The language should be simple, clear and communicate the message effectively. Helpline contact information should also be provided to give employees a chance to clarify if they have further questions around how to operate.

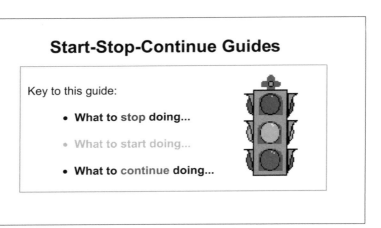

Figure 7.4   Start-stop-continue guides

In designing these guides, it is insufficient simply to translate them into the different languages required to cover the various geographies. It is likely that processes will have been delivered in very different ways across different geographies, and the guides will need to reflect this. In addition, the language used will need to vary across different cultures. It is important to produce appropriate templates, standards and examples of the outputs, and then to handover responsibility for the completion of the guides to local implementation teams, who have the prerequisite knowledge to complete the relevant details.

In the event these guides have been over-used in the organisation in the past, or have generated a poor track record in communicating change, an alternative way of presenting the key messages must be considered. The essential factor here is to get employees familiar with HR's service, and having them recognise how they can access it. An alternative approach to the stop-start-continue guide is what we call a Summary of Change Guide.

SUMMARY OF CHANGE GUIDES

The Summary of Change Guides (Figure 7.5) focus on summarising the differences in what activities staff need to complete, and what they will need to do differently.

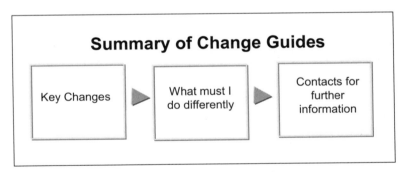

Figure 7.5   Summary of change guides

They provide a step-by-step guide to how to complete some of the key activities, what media or channels should be used, and how to get help through various media. Figure 7.6 provides examples of the type of information that these guides can contain.

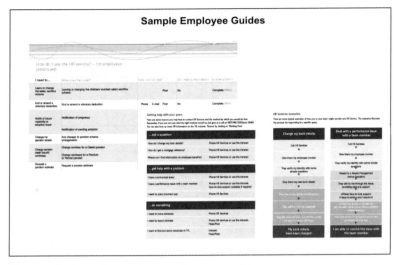

Figure 7.6   Sample employee guides

Creating and disseminating guides, regardless of the format they take, is only half the battle. Engaging effectively with key stakeholders, and delivering clear and concise communication as a precursor to the delivery of any 'training' interventions is key to a smooth and successful transition to your new global HR function.

⑧ Building a Cohesive Team

In setting up a global function, there is the inherent danger that the team itself will become fragmented, resulting in the gradual erosion of the use of standard tools and processes across the function, leading in turn to an overall degradation of service levels. Developed around a series of core specialisms, the structure does not lend itself to a natural progression through the HR function or knowledge sharing between teams, and end-to-end career paths are limited.

For example, the natural place to begin a career in HR would be within the Shared Service Centre (SSC). But the step from here to either the Centres of Excellence (CoE), or to become a Business Partner, is significant. Depth of technical expertise is essential within the centres of excellence but is not easily developed within the SSC, while the business knowledge and commercial acumen prerequisite for the business partner role demands experience in a business facing position rather than from within a back office function such as the SSC.

Other barriers to the development of a cohesive HR team include:

- *Distance*: The physical reach of an HR function can act as a significant barrier to cohesion. Work that is conducted in isolated groupings across a wide geography is often harder to monitor and direct. Further, communication and contact between HR practitioners is harder to achieve, for example HR employees in Thailand who have little contact with HR employees in Brazil are unlikely to associate themselves as a unified team.

- *Weak culture and brand*: Where the overall culture of the HR function is weak from the start, it is hard for the function to be distributed internationally and maintain any sense of cohesion. In these cases, the culture itself will tend to be overridden, in particular within local or regional operations. Values and beliefs are not widely shared, and again fragmentation of process, tools and brand will become an issue.

- *Variety of languages*: If employees are unable to communicate with each other, there is little chance for them to build relationships. With thousands of active languages, it is highly unlikely that (unless efforts are put in place to achieve this) all employees will speak the same language. Even when efforts are made to put a common language in place, for example in some banks English is used as the global language for communication, people may not be comfortable communicating within it, as they may lack certain vocabulary essentials. The issue here is that the power of communication is lost; even if employees are brought together, they are not able to communicate. Table 8.1 illustrates the potential size of this issue.

Table 8.1   Languages spoken globally

LOCATIONS	NUMBER OF LANGUAGES SPOKEN
Europe	230
Africa	+2,000
Middle East	72
India	+15
China	7

- **Cultural sensitivity**: Significant differences may exist across different cultures, which further contribute to the problem of building a cohesive team. For example, the paternalistic relationship of company to employee within Japan contrasts sharply with the United States, which represents a highly individualistic culture. Such differences represent further barriers to building a unified function.

None of these issues are insurmountable, nor in fact do they all need to be overcome. Once again, the theory of developing a single, unified team needs to be balanced against the reality of what is actually required by way of cohesion to ensure the global function operates effectively. For example, ensuring regular communication between Business Partners in France and colleagues in Japan may represent an ideal, but in practical terms is not a requirement for the overall delivery of an effective HR service.

HR BRAND

Building a strong HR brand is a powerful way of unifying your HR team. A brand defines who we are, what we deliver, what we believe, and how we behave and work. In defining a brand, it is important to:

- Establish the right culture.

- Develop commitment to quality and values.

- Create pride in delivery otherwise known as living the brand.

- Develop and sustain an environment of high quality and continuous improvement.

- Support leadership to manage and sustain the transformation.

- Create an environment of mutual trust and partnership.

In transforming to a global HR function, it is too easy to focus on the visible elements of the service (for example, processes, structures, systems) whilst ignoring the underlying factors that drive the overall brand. Figure 8.1 illustrates some of these underlying factors that need to be addressed specifically to deliver a consistent brand.

Key focus areas to developing a strong brand include:

- Creating a consistent global management and leadership style:

  - Setting clear expectations for HR leaders via a management competency framework to outline what good leaders and managers do.

- Establishing core management training which launches development of desired ways of working and behaviours for HR leadership and management.
- Establishing peer coaching networks to provide a practical means of developing HR management skills.
- Identifying key supervisors and managers to champion positive ways of managing.

• Using communication and development events to help HR staff refine their perception of the HR function regardless of where they are based geographically. This might include:

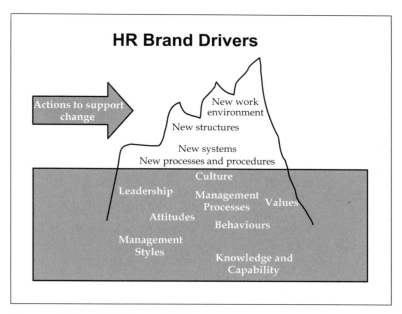

Figure 8.1   HR brand drivers

- Roadshows around the different regions to share positive and motivational messages to HR employees focussing on the strategic direction of HR and positioning HR as a 'great place to work'.
- Use of electronic forums such as chat rooms to communicate leadership views on the HR function, its direction and plans.

- Clarifying roles and ways of working across borders:

  - Often there are particular opportunity areas – certain roles where there is consistent dissatisfaction. In these cases, there are specific ways in which to improve satisfaction (such as rotations, on the job learning, personal development options, better definition of expectations).
  - Develop programmes to involve HR employees in understanding and solving problems in the organisation.

- Enhancing communication and involvement, particularly around positive changes and activities in the HR organisation, such as:

  - Launch materials and effective communication channels and media for the 'New HR' employer brand.
  - Build your employer brand through the HR website.
  - Develop links with the outside community through charitable activities, links with schools, thought leadership activities, publications and so on to create a positive image of the HR function in the wider community.

- Increasing support provided by HR processes and policies:

  - Identifying how HR processes and policies might be changed to better support HR employees, create the desired experience and support the brand values of HR. For example, establishing a performance management approach that supports desired ways of working.

- Making small but significant improvements to the working environment:

  - We have worked with HR teams to make small changes to the work environment and introduce flexibility to work arrangements to enable employees to fit work around their personal commitments and to fully concentrate on work when they are there.

Having established the brand, it is important to ensure HR teams understand how they can make a difference to the employee experience of HR, and therefore improve the customer's perception of HR.

The aim here is to motivate HR staff to be committed, responsible and responsive – to do all they can to deliver the HR promise to customers and become ambassadors of the brand. This will help HR staff to recognise the need to raise the game above past performance of customer service, to exceed customer expectations and to reflect the brand everyday in the actions of everything they do at work. By undertaking this work, the consistency of service provision across the global stage can be significantly enhanced.

Any work of this kind needs to be carefully integrated with ongoing initiatives to improve service delivery, such as process improvement exercises or definition of service delivery standards.

In seeking to build on its HR brand, a global player within the Oil and Gas industry decided to improve the customer experience of HR, firstly by helping HR staff to experience what it felt like to be a customer, and secondly to play an active role in improving that experience. Figure 8.2 illustrates the model they used.

1) UNDERSTANDING THE CUSTOMER EXPERIENCE

The team employed a number of interventions to heighten HR staff's understanding of the customer experience. These included:

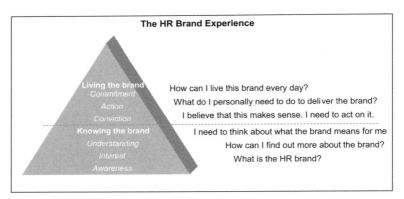

The HR Brand Experience

Living the brand
Commitment
Action
Conviction

How can I live this brand every day?
What do I personally need to do to deliver the brand?
I believe that this makes sense. I need to act on it.

Knowing the brand
Understanding
Interest
Awareness

I need to think about what the brand means for me
How can I find out more about the brand?
What is the HR brand?

Figure 8.2   The HR brand experience

- Facilitating customer experience simulations demonstrating the impact that HR employees can have, to ensure empathy with customer expectations by using a moments of truth framework (critical, but often apparently small events which greatly impact the customer experience positively or negatively).

- Role plays and simulation workshops (using actors where appropriate) to put HR employees in customers' shoes. These created stories that passed through the HR organisation grapevine through the use of informal networks that further bolstered the brand.

- Analysis and observation of customer experience at every point of contact with the organisation.

- Review of current data, such as customer satisfaction surveys, to understand priority customer issues.

2) IMPROVING THE CUSTOMER EXPERIENCE

The team employed a number of interventions to change the employee experience of HR consistently across the global function. The focus was on helping HR staff to understand how they could influence the customer experience and not dwell on issues that were beyond their control. They included:

- Establishing a new HR exhibition, which toured globally and that enabled HR employees to see and experience changes to the employee experience and showcase the changes in the HR function that supported superior customer service.

- The design and launch of global workforce action teams, face-to-face or via the intranet. These were forums for HR people who were actually working on and impacted by activities and processes, and focused on improving them. The self-organising teams worked within a framework on issues that were important to them and which directly or indirectly improved customer service.

- Use of communication and new HR champions to spread the word. These were key HR leads and managers who could tap into informal networks and could model positive behaviour and ways of working.

- Use of a newly developed global behaviour/competency framework (building on existing frameworks where appropriate) which defined behaviour and which supported customer satisfaction, performance, HR employee satisfaction and cost effectiveness.

Table 8.2 provides a summary of some of the tactics that may be used to build a cohesive HR team.

GOVERNANCE AND REPORTING STRUCTURES THAT SUPPORT THE HR TEAM

Once you have established the structure of the new global HR model, there is a risk that you may pay insufficient attention to establishing the underlying governance and reporting structures that will enable the new function to work as a single team.

Table 8.2 Tactics to support 'one team'

Tactic	Example
Global Branding for the transformed HR	Values and mission statements need to be developed and articulated to the HR employees
Unify HR outputs	Standardise the outputs of HR such as forms and documents to give HR a standard and consistent global identity
Annual conferences where people are united	Bringing people together can help the HR organisation to build the relationships globally
Internal campaigns of 'one-ness'	Devising social events to build supportive relationships between different segments of HR organisation
Job rotation-ex pat movement	Job rotation will help to build relationships and disseminate best practice and promote knowledge sharing
Have an inspirational HRD to lead	Having inspirational leadership will help to motivate HR staff and would help them to identify with the transformed HR
Play up on companies history	To encourage employees to identify with the company
Outline service standards with KPIs/benchmarks in place (and someone in charge of benchmarks)	Measuring services and processes to increase HR's credibility within the global organisation

One of the biggest challenges for successful global HR is the fragmentation of the function. Business Partners, policy experts and employees in SSCs will quickly develop the habit of operating in silos and ignoring the other roles within their function, unless specific interventions are put in place to mitigate against this. Adding global operations into the mix exacerbates this risk.

The creation of appropriate and clear reporting structures between and within different components is very important. Effective channels are important not just from a basic reporting and management perspective but also because they can enable the sharing of best practice for continued improvement.

To achieve this, it is useful to define key stakeholders who are essential to effective communication. These may include the heads of different groups of Business Partners, CoE, and SSC leads. Their role is not only to send and receive information, but to ensure they keep their teams updated with the knowledge and communication they receive. Figure 8.3 shows how communication and reporting can be structured both vertically and horizontally.

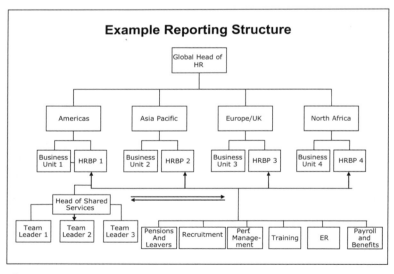

Figure 8.3   Example reporting structure

There is no one right design for the governance model of a global HR function. Rather it is a question of balancing business requirements together with local and global needs. When defining your governance model, you should address the following questions:

- Do HR Business Partners directly report into the Global Head of Business Partners?

- Does Shared Services report/communicate the proper information to the CoE to help them to devise appropriate HR policy?

- Do the CoE have enough contact with Business Partners to strike a balance between policy making that is legal and compliant and policy making to meet business needs?

- Do the various Shared Service hubs have leaders that communicate with each other worldwide?

- Is the organisational design flexible enough to allow for job rotation between the different components?

In support of the governance structure, a clear global communication plan should be developed for HR. This should define the channels, frequency, relevant audiences, objectives and key content of the various global communication media. This plan should be integrated with regional and local plans, to ensure seamless, end-to-end communications are in place.

CLARITY OF ACCOUNTABILITY

Hand in hand with the creation of an effective governance model goes the clear articulation of roles, responsibilities and accountabilities within the global target operating model. The need to articulate clearly what everyone does to ensure the delivery of an effective service becomes doubly important when operating at a global level.

Each unit must understand their accountabilities and what their respective roles and responsibilities entail. Role descriptions are basic but powerful tools for capturing and communicating what a certain HR role involves and where the role and responsibilities start and finish. In the following example (Figure 8.4) we provide you with a template which has been tested with multiple clients and has proved to be effective in communicating HR's new roles in the transformed function.

Having established global roles, it is important that these are kept up to date (and in particular in line with any changes to the organisation chart and underlying governance structure). They should be accessible to all HR staff, for example via the global HR intranet.

SUMMARY

Here is a list of our top eight tips for encouraging integration across a global HR team:

1. Hire staff with a globally adaptable mindset.

Role Description	
Job Title: **Reports to:** **Pay band:**	
Purpose and Scope	
• Describe in high level what the role is set out to achieve.	
Accountable For	
• List of key accountabilities.	
Major Activities	
• Scope of involvement (for example, Strategy Development, Development and Management of staff).	
Organisation Chart	
• The global reporting structure in a diagrammatic format.	
Key Performance Indicators	
• Quantitative and qualitative measures of success.	
Areas of Authority for Decision-Making	
• **Key decision-making powers:** • **Constraints:** • **Financial impact:** • **Employees:** Number of employees that the role is in charge of. • **Other information:**	
Key Interfaces	
Key stakeholders that the role relates to.	

Figure 8.4   Sample role description template

2. Deliver training interventions that enable interactions with colleagues from across the world.

3. Establish global teams and projects to develop ties between HR colleagues across borders, geographies and business units.

4. Exploit technology as an international link.

5. Rotate the locations for important meetings to develop a global mindset.

6. Immerse staff in foreign locations through expatriate programmes.

7. Institute a culturally diverse global HR leadership team to help build a global mindset.

8. Cultivate a set of core HR values, or brand, throughout the function.

(9) Delivering HR Talent

Sustaining the effective delivery of value-added service within any HR function, be it local, regional or global in reach, is dependent on the skills, capability and capacity of the HR team members themselves. The Corporate Leadership Council has found that developing talent within HR departments has a greater contribution to the effectiveness of HR than changing structure or building IT technologies (Table 9.1). The growth and maintenance of talent is therefore a critical activity for the HR function.

Table 9.1   Developing talent to deliver effectiveness

HR Improvement Strategy	Contribution to Effectiveness
HR talent development	29%
Changing structure	13%
IT technology	9%

There are a number of challenges for the delivery of global talent programmes. These include:

- Lack of integrated systems and data to support the identification and management of talent.

- Lack of defined end-to-end career paths within the HR structure, in particular as a result of the degree of specialism inherent within the Ulrich model.

- Achieving the right balance between local and regionally-driven talent initiatives, and global talent activities.

- Language barriers associated with the global deployment of talent.

- Issues associated with the delivery of global development programmes, for example, cultural differences.

- Variations in education levels and professional qualifications across the global HR population.

- Challenges associated with the global deployment of talent, for example, financial costs and language issues.

- Generating globally applicable criteria to define talent.

None of these challenges are insurmountable. However, they are significant enough to mean that careful consideration must be taken in deciding at what level talent management will be driven globally, and what activities will be retained at a local or regional level.

IDENTIFYING THE TALENT POOL AND KEY POSITIONS

The first step in any talent initiative involves the identification of the talent pool and the key positions which will feature in the succession plan. Typically, organisations will define talent as the top 10–15 per cent of staff within the organisation. Organisations that run truly global talent activities are extremely rare however. While in a regional or locally-based HR function, a key question will be at what structural level talent management will be applied. Within a global HR function the key question is at what structural level will talent be managed globally, rather than locally or regionally?

You need to develop a consistent set of criteria that defines talent. These criteria must be consistent at both a local/regional level and a global level. Where possible, the criteria should link in to any global competencies that are in place. However, the absence of a global competency framework need not preclude the creation of a robust set of talent criteria which can be used in lieu of competency-based data.

The other set of criteria which need to be set at a consistent level between the global and local/regional levels are the criteria that define what represents a key position within the organisation. Use of such criteria ensures that only critical roles are included in the succession plan and where the organisation structure of HR changes, a set of principles exists against which new roles can be assessed.

There are two elements that are important to the identification of both the talent pool and the key positions:

- Development of a 'Talent Forum' or committee, who will drive talent activities across the HR function, and arbitrate on important decisions, such as: the exact criteria to be used to signify talent; the assessments that will be used to identify talent; and the criteria that will define what represents a key position within the overall succession plan. Within a global function, it is important to ensure the membership represents the different functional areas within HR, as well as the different geographies within the group. Business representatives should be included in the group to ensure a customer-focused perspective is maintained. Ideally, members of this group should hold key roles within the functional or geographic talent committees that drive local/regional activities.

- Creation of a global talent bank, used to store all the essential information needed to track and manage the knowledge and skills of your HR function worldwide. To manage talent successfully on a global scale, it is vital that your HR function has a shared system to keep this knowledge centrally, while having it accessible to all. This may entail a centrally used HR portal. The purpose of a global talent bank is not only to use your employees' abilities to maximise the needs of your global organisation, but to have a plan for how to fill future talent gaps that may be identified in any office worldwide. Data to record includes:

  - Language capability.
  - Qualifications, presentation skills, facilitation skills, and project management skills.
  - Educational achievements.
  - Measurements of performance.
  - International experience.
  - In-house and external training records.
  - Past employment records.
  - History of global deployment.

Data ownership is also a critical factor in effective management of the talent pool.

Data can be captured from the point where an HR employee is first recruited; curriculum vitae and standard online application procedures can help to start this list. Where possible, self-service should be used, so the employees themselves are responsible for their own data, with line management completing a validation/verification role. For instance, when an employee completes a training programme, they can update their profile through the employee self-service. Subsequently, when a line manager finishes their performance reviews, this can also be entered to the system through manager self-service. Key to the success of this process is establishment of globally held data ownership and maintenance principles. It is essential that there is a clear agreement of who can enter which information. We also recommended regular check points to ensure proper maintenance standards.

A key purpose of maintaining a global talent database is to track talent efficiently worldwide. A common downfall of global HR functions is their inability to keep up-to-date on the skills different employees possess. In worse case scenarios, they will hire external duplicate skills, as they are unaware of employees in their organisation who possess these skills. Maintenance of up-to-date talent pool data helps to map out quickly where the global HR function is in terms of qualifications and skill sets. By providing such information, it helps HR to assess whether the right skill sets exist for the company. This, in turn, helps HR to plan its resourcing strategy such as when it is appropriate to develop and recruit employees. By analysing such data, you can understand employees' strengths and weaknesses and plan their development in an informed and systematic way.

SUCCESSION AND CAREER PLANNING

The succession planning activity should occur regularly, for example quarterly, across the function. Local, regional (or functional) and global succession planning activities must be scheduled to an agreed calendar, to ensure that talent is able to cross over from one talent pool to another. Regular sessions also ensure that talent is identified in a timely manner, and the succession plan can be updated with the right target staff at appropriate intervals.

The Talent Forum or committee has a key role in updating the succession plan. Based on the assessment information provided, they must take decisions as to the best candidates to fill the key organisational roles within HR, and ensure there is a pipeline of talent available to staff future capability requirements. This activity is of particular importance in banks and other regulated organisations, where documented evidence of effective talent planning is a regulatory requirement.

As part of this process, the Talent Forum should also consider whether career paths within the organisation are appropriate and lend themselves to building the right type of experience needed to produce candidates of the right calibre. Where this is not the case, specific actions must be identified to develop initiatives that will mitigate the situation, for example the development of new career paths, opportunities for cross-functional sabbaticals, or international or expatriate work schemes.

MENTORING, COACHING AND DEVELOPMENT

Having identified the target individuals who map to the key roles on the succession plan, specific interventions need to be developed to coach and develop those individuals. Again, where development programmes are to be delivered on a global basis, careful consideration must be given to the design and content of the programmes, if they are to be appropriate to a geographically and functionally mixed audience.

In developing such programmes, the following checklist (Figure 9.1) can be useful in testing the appropriateness of materials.

TRAINING SAFETY CHECKLIST	
Participants	Balance: is there a right balance in terms of levels of knowledge and skills among the participants? Gender balance: is it appropriate to deliver training as a mixed sex group?
Training Material	Use of images in training material: are symbols culturally sensitive? The level of language: is the language accessible to global operations? Cultural sensitivity: does the training material avoid cultural stereotypes? Balance in terms of learning styles: is the training material appropriate for staff with different learning preferences (visual, audio, experiential)?
Learning Style	Direct Role-play Workshops Coaching
Assessment of Training	Self-completed questionnaires: does the training. meet objectives? Did the training help to meet KPIs?

Figure 9.1   Training safety checklist

Similarly, evaluation of global programmes should encompass three levels (Figure 9.2).

EVALUATION OF TRAINING PROGRAMMES	
Organisational	To what extent are the business benefits of the training programme underpinned by the increased effectiveness of the HR staff? To what extent have service performance measures been achieved?
Functional	How successful has the development programme been as a mechanism for: • Building HR bench strength? • Retaining core skills? • Integrating the function?
Individual	Individual and line manager assessment against competencies required. Assessment of success in driving the appropriate change in behaviours.

Figure 9.2   Evaluation of training checklist

Once more, the degree of globalisation required needs to be carefully considered when developing such interventions. It may be desirable to use coaches or mentors from different geographies to reinforce the global culture of HR, but in practical terms this may not be feasible. Most organisations working on a global basis achieve a balance of global and local support, using global training interventions to foster *one* culture, while taking advantage of local management structures to provide effective mentoring and support. Achieving this balance will be important to sustaining your global HR function.

⑩ Global HR Metrics

KEY CONSIDERATIONS

HR metrics are used to monitor the performance of an HR function. The aim is to measure the effectiveness of the HR strategy and to provide key management information for workforce planning and improvement. Metrics serve more than one purpose; on the one hand, they give a current and accurate assessment of how your HR function is delivering, and on the other hand, can be used to build future improvements and efficiencies. The main difference when deploying use of metrics across a global function is that the range of variables to measure increases, as does the level of complexity involved in capturing accurate and comparable data.

In a global HR function it is not uncommon to find multiple Shared Service Centres (SSC) and Centres of Expertise that are linked to diverse business units in a large number of regions. In this case, it is very possible that there will be different service requirements for different regional businesses, adding a layer of complexity to data collation and analysis. Differences in the core processes can result in the need for different metrics.

For example, managing exit processes can be very different in Germany and the United States as a result of the involvement of employee representation bodies in the former, Comparing these two processes by way of metrics can often become meaningless because of the very different nature of the processes themselves. As this example illustrates, a key consideration for developing metrics in global HR function/organisation is deciding the extent to which they will be globally integrated and locally differentiated.

In defining global metrics, key considerations include:

- *Obtaining a global-local balance*: Global firms must consistently monitor and measure both how they are performing globally, as well as the success of each of their regions. Successful metrics in global operations requires a balance of the two.

- *Understanding comparability of data*: The ability to evaluate data comparably between regions is not always possible. For this reason it is essential to decide which metrics between regions are comparable, as well as which ones are unique.

- *Scrutinising geographic dispersion*: Differences in location, time and language often complicate the ability to understand if specific regional performance is consistent with the rest of the organisation. It is the role of the HR function to overcome this.

- *Maintaining flexibility*: The key to a successful approach to metrics in a global function is contingent on flexibility. Flexibility is essential as the metric framework deployed must 'fit' a variety of solutions worldwide extending way beyond national boundaries.

SELECTING THE RIGHT METRICS

Selecting the right metrics for a global function is difficult. It is essential to select measures that:

- Are most strongly correlated with success in the business;

- Are within the capability of existing systems to measure;

- Have data available (if externally benchmarking).

In addition, it is important to select a number of measures such that:

- Major value drivers and strategic priorities are represented;

- Tell a story of business performance;

- They do not create confusion and unnecessary work.

In defining metrics it is important to develop a hierarchy of measures which will populate an overall balanced scorecard. Figure 10.1 shows the different levels that typically make up a scorecard, together with the different objectives of each level.

Typically in most global HR functions, the starting point for building a balanced score card is rethinking and clarifying the HR business strategy. This process involves highlighting the global HR function's key value creation areas (or key result areas – KRA) and directing a strategy based upon them.

Service management framework – example			
Type	Definition	Example	Reported
Key Result Area (KRA)	Service Line mission statement	L&D – Ensure employees are equipped with the skills and knowledge required to meet their job and development needs	Not reported – a guiding principle
Key Performance Indicators (KPI)	Measure and continually reviewed target that evaluates and directs Group HR Services contribution to business performance	Recruiting – Cost per recruit	Reported and reviewed with clients
Service Level Agreements (SLA)	Measure and continually reviewed target of cusomter experience and/or quality	Customer Services – All calls will be answered within 20 seconds	May be reported if significant for a period
Operating Level Agreements (OLA)	Measure and continually reviewed target of input required by parties external to HRS in order to execute a process	Reward – Input overtime hours before cut-off	May be reported if significant for a period
Efficiency Measures (EM)	Measure and continually reviewed target of internal HRS performance	Customer Services – Ratio of call centre agents to calls	SSC Internal reporting only

Figure 10.1   Service management framework

HR can then select the key metrics and build up a scorecard that is consistent with and clearly represents the aims identified. The metrics typically range from basic efficiency measures, to operating and service level agreements, to the actual Key Performance Indicators (KPI) that measure the HR function's contribution to business performance. Each KPI should represent the best indicator of performance for a specific Key Result Area (KRA) and every KRA should have at least one measure.

Finally, having established KPIs, performance standards are identified which represent the ideal level of performance. Tracking performance measures over time enables HR professionals to understand which areas need attention.

It is then HR's role to implement and measure the critical factors identified through the means of collecting, collating and measuring data, and compiling this into the overall balanced scorecard.

Table 10.1 provides a framework to guide the creation of metrics. It includes examples which we have used in the past to help our clients build up their working scorecard. It is important to note that in a global HR function, strategic KRAs, KPIs and Performance Standards often vary by region.

Table 10.1   Performance metrics

Dimension	KRAs	KPIs	Performance Standards
Strategic	Attract and retain talent Build strategic capabilities Cleary defined cultures and values Provision of strategic management info	Retention of high performers Development of core programmes Accuracy/timeliness of management information	95% new hires retention for six months 90% skills attainment 85% employee satisfaction % accuracy and turnaround time
Customer	Partner with business Provide responsive quality service	Customer satisfaction rates	80% time spent with execs 90% customer satisaction
Operations	Optimise HR services through service delivery model	Volume per delivery channel Cost per transaction Average cycle times	% query resolution by channel 95% self-service take-up
Financial	Maximise human capital performance Minimise HR costs	HR ROI HR cost per FTE	1% HR cost to revenue £1000 per employee head 0.5% budget variance

However, the extent to which they differ is contingent upon the level of maturity of the business and its priorities.

For example, for one particular region, a high retention rate for employees (due to the lack of required specific skills within their workforce) may be the key factor for HR to measure. In another region this may not be relevant, whereas the measurement of the number of payroll errors such as overcompensation may be critical.

KEY QUESTIONS IN BUILDING A GLOBAL HR SERVICE MANAGEMENT FRAMEWORK

Important questions you should consider include:

- Customer perspective: what do HR's customers need? How can HR provide this?

- Key processes: what are the key processes that create value for achieving business strategy?

- Internal processes: how can HR ensure their service is as effective and efficient as possible?

- Learning and growth (or innovation): what can HR do to achieve the organization's vision?

Other key questions include:

- What metrics should our global function measure to address the above questions?

- What is unique about how our HR function is organised that really brings value to the business?

- How can we get the information we need to measure?

- What data should we benchmark ourselves against?

- How can we present our measured findings to bring most value to:

  - Variety of regions?
  - Functional units of HR?
  - Business units?

THE BALANCED SCORECARD

The balanced scorecard provides critical information to management regarding HR's key performance metrics. It generally presents data from the service management framework with intuitive symbols such as traffic lights and directional arrows to inform and indicate areas within HR that are on track, as well as ones that require attention. Balanced scorecards can also be used to measure the performance of specific HR processes through metrics.

By breaking down performance in a global HR function, be it by service, functional unit (Business Partners, SSC, Policy experts), or by region, it is possible to monitor where HR is in terms of its overall effectiveness and efficiency. The most important role that metrics serve (which is often forgotten), is their practical application to informing key business decisions, regardless of whether your organisation is considering furthering their expansion efforts, or just looking to understand its current state. By providing numerical information, global metrics help to link the long-term strategic measures of a firm to short- term financial measures.

THE IMPORTANCE OF BUSINESS FEEDBACK

The success of a global HR function must be measured not only on the basis of numbers and ratios between regions, but also on the quality of the service it provides to the business. HR truly creates value when it satisfies its customers.

Surveying business users on their satisfaction with the services that they receive from HR is still a relatively new phenomenon. However, research suggests that there is a positive link between levels of employee satisfaction with internal functions such as HR, and overall business performance. By asking employees to quantify their satisfaction with various HR services (for example, training and development, compensation and benefits), HR can form a view of the areas of HR that require improvement.

In a global HR function, it is essential to measure this on a global scale, but to also have the flexibility to break responses down by region to allow for comparisons by region. In our experience with building metrics in a global HR function, feedback is gathered not only to determine satisfaction levels overall but to benchmark regions against each other to look for improvement. The grey area in this process is seeking to identify if successful ratings in one region are due to exceptional service or to cultural reactions to being surveyed (that is, generally positive responses). The output of these surveys is often useful in making the business feel like it has been listened to and that its voice matters.

WHAT ARE THE PITFALLS IN BUILDING AND USING METRICS FOR GLOBAL COMPANIES?

- *Measuring metrics inconsistently across regions*: Measuring metrics inconsistently across different regions can potentially be a real problem inhibiting the use of effective global metrics. The underlying cause for this is the fact that metric reports are delivered by different people at different points of time. This problem raises questions about how the data is derived, and can undermine the reliability of the process overall.

- *Lack of understanding and interpretation of results*: The key problem here lies in the misinterpretation of metrics by key business users around the world. This arises most often from a lack of consistent use of language and terms, leading to a misinterpretation of information in a global function. However, even when language is not an issue, there is also the potential that data users often have a limited understanding of the scope of metrics and what they are set out to achieve. This is because in a global HR function, the people who collate and measure the data are often very far removed from those that analyse it. Users of metrics should have a shared belief of what qualifies a good versus a bad metric result.

- *Poorly aligning with your audience when producing results*: Data needs to be shared with the right audience. Producing a number of different reports and dashboards may be appropriate for different audiences. For instance, executives, Business Partners, Heads of SSCs and line managers in different regions often require varying levels of detailed information.

- *Not using metrics data for decision making*: No matter how accurately metrics capture what is happening in an organisation, if they are not used to make key decisions the effort to collect them is wasted. This is often the case when a lack of trust permeates throughout the organisation, or the culture of decision making is more about 'guess and test' than evidenced-based decision making. To avoid the former, it is important to have a process of checking data accuracy to increase the credibility of metrics encouraging their use.

Our top six tips for using metrics effectively in a global organisation are:

1. Clarify what the measure means as well as its purpose. Based on the variety of perceptions and interpretations that exist in a global HR function, when it comes to metrics it is essential to agree on a common understanding of the metrics selected, and how they are to be measured and interpreted.

2. Define standards for measurement. Although it is inevitable that some measures will take a regional focus in a global organisation, those chosen to be used across the entire organisation must be measured consistently. This requires that a methodology be disseminated across the globally dispersed HR function outlining exactly what is to be measured and how this information is to be gathered.

3. Encourage a single best way for measurement. Make sure employees in the HR function involved in the collation and analysis of metrics are appropriately trained. Build this into a development programme and communicate it as a top priority.

4. Identify common data sources and maintenance principles. It is important to identify common sources of data such as a payroll system or an HRIS. It is also recommended that procedures for checking data and assigning responsibility for doing so are set.

5. Create a culture that values metrics. To utilise the power of metrics fully it is important to build a culture in which people are encouraged to rely on hard evidence. It is equally important to be committed to fact-based decision making. This requires a commitment to getting the best evidence and using it to guide actions.

6. Be flexible. Business priorities often change based on both internal and external conditions, and often within a short time span. Take a flexible approach that accommodates shifting priorities always ensuring your metrics reflect the parallel changes.

SUMMARY

- HR metrics help to assess the performance of an HR function. The value lies in providing key management information for workforce planning and improvement.

- Achieving a global-local balance when defining metrics is key, together with understanding the comparability of data, scrutinising geographic dispersion and maintaining flexibility. Flexibility is essential as the metric framework deployed must 'fit' a variety of solutions worldwide extending way beyond national boundaries.

- Building a balanced scorecard for a global HR involves a number of stages. A crucial step here is gaining an understanding of the organisations' key value creation areas, together with its' short- and long-term objectives. Once this is achieved, you then need to identify the key human capital deliverables and the strategic behaviours and competencies that enable the workforce to create value. The next step is the selection of the key HR metrics themselves.

- The most common barriers to the effective use of global HR metrics are inconsistencies in measurement across regions, lack of understanding of and inconsistent interpretation of results by key stakeholders, and not using the results in decision making. Building a culture in which people make evidence-based decisions is vital.

- These issues can be tackled by clarifying what the measures mean and gaining agreement on a common understanding of the metrics selected, and how they are to be measured and interpreted.

PART III
Case Studies and Conclusions

⑪ Case Studies

The following case studies were selected to highlight how this book's four issues have played out in reality. They demonstrate how, if these key issues are addressed properly, HR functions can become global in their reach. The cases seek to bring these issues to life, demonstrating how these example organisations have sought to overcome them in their efforts to achieve successfully operating global HR functions.

HOW GE CAPITAL HAS USED HR TO BECOME GLOBAL

GE Capital is a legendary example of a once local, USA based, organisation that, by exploiting their HR function, has mastered the art of global expansion. By way of mergers and acquisitions GE Capital has successfully achieved global status. In 1996 alone, their revenue grew more than 27 per cent from $518 billion to $658.8 billion. With over 100 acquisitions in 5 years, they have increased their workforce by 30 per cent, doubled their net income, globalised their business, and of course, globalised their HR department. They call it their 'urge to merge' and have tailored the process to an art form.

But how do they do it? Knowing that many organisations fail in their M&A efforts, what is it that makes GE Capital successful?

GE Capital is a pioneer in its efforts to look beyond financial facts to examine the potential synergy between two organisations – to the extent that they have been known to abolish a plan to integrate if there is no clear fit. If they decide to progress, they thoroughly assess the level of integration that is required. According to GE Capital's track record in going global, there are four types of M&As:

1. Asset purchase: add value to a particular business.

2. Consolidating acquisitions: company is purchased and integrated into GE Capital.

3. Acquisition to move into fresh territory.

4. Hybrid with some parts fitting into existing business and the rest is left as a joint venture.

In examining their M&A process, it is obvious that the success experienced is in large part based on HR's due diligence efforts. HR is the glue that holds their international expansion efforts together. This focus on HR due diligence is particularly unusual. Most organisations typically focus solely on the financial aspects of a transaction; with any HR data reviewed generally relating to the total salary bill, pension commitments, and executive bonus and package.

At GE Capital, from the offset they first seek to answer the golden question – can the two organisations and their cultures potentially fit together? If the decision is made to go ahead,

HR then selects a full-time integration manager to create the connective tissue between the two organisations, as well as to integrate plans and targets. They must be experienced, know the business well, and possess great interpersonal skills.

HR continues to have a role throughout the rest of the process. They help communicate the merger news to the rest of the organisation with the aim of reducing uncertainty. Further down the line, HR holds a strategic role in helping to select which talent should remain in the case of duplicate roles. They provide coaching to employees in need and help identify training needs for new members of their team, be it through an external course or internally through Capital University.

SCHRODERS: MANAGEMENT OF PROCESS IN A GLOBAL FUNCTION

After an extensive review was carried out to investigate the workings of the local UK HR function, it was realised that the HR activities performed locally could potentially be rolled out globally. Due to the development of activities worldwide, there was a need to assess how various local operations could be rethought in order to ensure the most effective service was being delivered. From discussions with regional HR representatives it was obvious that adopting a new service model where a number of HR processes could be managed globally would be beneficial.

To understand the success of globally managed HR processes, an investigation was completed to identify which HR processes were already being managed on a global level. It was discovered that there was a theme of globally managed HR processes including:

- Headcount reporting.

- Performance management.

- International assignments.

- Compensation.

- Senior resourcing.

- Talent management/identification.

The potential to expand the global management of processes was discussed by the HR leadership, at an offsite working session. This allowed regional representatives to work together to identify several candidate processes and debate the consequences of managing them globally. By the close of the offsite it was agreed that the key obstacle to delivering a number of processes globally was lack of an integrated single HR information system and database. Following the implementation of such a system, it was agreed that a number of other important processes could be managed globally. These included:

- Absence management.

- Job evaluation.

- Position management.

- New joiner processes, including induction.

- Recruitment approvals.

- All management information requests/standard reporting using a common employee data model.

During the initial transition period to the new HRIS, the project team was also in charge of reviewing how and when these processes would be migrated to a global service delivery model, and what this would mean for the regional HR teams as well as the impact on the London based organisation. It was decided that despite the fact that many processes worldwide would continue to be managed locally, they must report data globally for management information needs.

Despite the global management of key processes, it was decided that there was not a need for 24-hour service support for any global process administered from the UK, although this would need to be confirmed with regional HR teams. It was identified that it there would be a need for 24-hour service support for the global HRIS system.

SHELL'S EFFORT TO UNIFY THEIR FUNCTION

Shell is an example of a global organisation that has made a considerable effort to unify its HR function worldwide. As a starting point to achieve this, Shell exploited the concept of global HR branding. The brand, HR Excellence, sought to encourage all HR employees worldwide to identify to a common idea of what HR represents and how they should operate. The brand was based on the idea that talent is Shell's number one HR priority, both within their function and for the rest of the organisation. Each local HR function conformed to the overall brand values and sought to apply the brand locally.

Shell has operations in over 145 countries, with an HR function of 3,000, servicing a client base of 115,000. The brand itself and what it means to be part of HR at Shell is reinforced by its use of IT – in particular the company's HRIS tool. By the end of 2004, over two-thirds of Shell employees worldwide began using the HRIS tool. Named 'Shell People Services system', it is one of the largest and most visible SAP-HR systems. The HRIS combines process improvement, introduction of a single global solution, and paves the way for future global HR services across Shell that are consistent across countries and continents.

Shell's global HR function is unique in the sense that it is staffed with a range of employees worldwide that all think of themselves as global in scope and perspective. All or most functions and business units operate on a truly global basis – they are not simply aggregates of independent local entities. As a global organisation, they expect their HR professionals to work with global teams. This serves as another way of unifying HR, for by working together worldwide, connections between HR employees in different counties worldwide begin to develop. This is complemented with expatriate and employee movement, so HR employees working in one region understand what it is like to work in another region. Once an employee is hired, they are most likely to be moved globally and gain further exposure to the common brand.

ZEGNA'S APPROACH TO TALENT MANAGEMENT

Developing from a local family business operating in Italy, Zegna's reach quickly extended globally, with operations across the Asia Pacific, Europe and North America. This change created the need for a more reliable and value-adding HR function. The effects of rapid expansion were felt as Zegna quickly transformed from an organisation requiring little HR support to one in need of proper management. As the company was moving towards a more performance-led culture, HR needed to demonstrate performance and deliverables as a priority. HR was meant to set an example for the rest of the organisation but to do so they required the proper talent to set the bar.

To transform themselves and start the in-house talent trend, HR looked to bring in talent at the top. To make the switch from a local model, small-scale family operating business to fit their global operations required a thorough assessment of in-house knowledge and ability. With a lack of leadership binding the function together, a global head of HR was recruited. The choice was a woman from outside Italy, someone with not only a deep level of expertise, but a fresh perspective on how to organise the HR function. They didn't stop there.

With a strong executive planting the seeds for the future function, other knowledgeable HR professionals were essential to reflect and enable her vision. Training and developing talent became the major levers for transforming HR to meet the changing demands of the organisation. The global HR director has gone as far as to mandate this approach, starting with HR and extending it throughout the rest of the organisation.

Despite the increase in externally recruited HR talent, there was a strong need at Zegna to have HR demonstrating their value, especially with reference to demonstrating the commercial acumen and business contribution of HR. Business Partners needed to establish themselves as effective co-workers with management. As the company moved to a more performance-led culture, there was a need for HR to demonstrate their achievements to the rest of the business.

Efforts to manage and retain talent have included the implementation of bi-annual HR workshops. The role of these workshops is to enhance pragmatic thought within the global HR function, as well as to develop talent and capability. To tailor the development needs of the employees, the workshops focus on the new skills employees are expected to possess. These have included:

- Business planning.

- The ability to identify and drive forward initiatives.

- The development of new skills based on skills gaps.

- Knowledge and understanding of HR systems and process.

- Understanding the importance and relevance of tracking and measuring progress.

This HR talent initiative at Zegna is not reserved to learning at the bi-annual workshops. The development of talent in HR business partners at Zegna is ongoing, where employees are given the opportunity to practice their skills daily. It is believed that a huge part of the learning curve is based on successful interactions with their business units which enhance their confidence, coaching, facilitation and feedback skills.

(12) Conclusion

Changes in technology over the last 20 years have opened the door for organisations to globalise operations. Operational changes vary from simply leveraging economies of scale, such as centralising and standardising low value processes, to expanding global footprint to take advantage of new markets, cheaper production and the opportunity to leverage specialisations to deliver differentiated offerings on a global basis.

The challenge and issues associated with transforming your HR function to support this activity cannot be underestimated, and places a new demand on the skills of HR professionals responsible for delivering such change. Outsourcing, offshoring, the implementation of global HR systems and processes, maintaining a cohesive brand and team, and building global HR talent are just a few of the activities HR leadership has to focus on going forward.

Within this book, we have provided some practical guidelines and suggestions to help HR leadership in delivering a successful HR service to their organisation. The service itself may range from a mix of local and regional focus, to a full global HR model. There is no single right answer in terms of how far along the route to globalisation an HR function should go: rather the solution lies in achieving the right balance of global to regional/local focus, in line with the overall strategy of the organisation and the natural constraints that exist within this field. We have reviewed some of the debates surrounding globalisation, focused on some of the issues and pitfalls that may arise along the way, cited examples and case studies of work other organisations have completed in this field, and provided tools that can be used to facilitate HR transformation within a global context.

The vision for HR is important to developing a function capable of supporting a global organisation. Clarity of outcomes and the principles used to define solutions are critical, and the tools and approach outlined in this guide can be used to support such transformation, whether it be in terms of developing basic global capability, or a full global HR model.

Orion Partners

Orion Partners are leading independent advisers in HR Transformation. Established in 2002, we have led and managed HR Transformation programmes for over 30 blue chip clients and our client base covers leading organisations in both private and public sectors.

We help organisations to succeed in their HR transformation by enabling them to:

- Clarify and define HR's strategy and role relative to the business.

- Decide on the most suitable operating model for HR, including the option of shared services or outsourcing.

- Select and implement the right technology solutions.

- Assess and select the right people.

- Develop the skills and mindset to succeed.

- Make the transformation happen on the ground.

Our unique focus is the whole range of HR transformation activities. We pride ourselves on the independence and practical nature of our advice and our focus on identifying and capturing the benefits in our design and implementation. We have skills and expertise in scoping, design and change management of the transition.

We have a have a broad base of functional, industry and global experience. Together with deep knowledge of HR and what makes it work successfully. We undertake regular research in the HR field including our unique studies on the difference that makes a difference in HR Business partners and HR Leaders.

If you would like to find out more, please visit www.orion-partners.com or call us on +44 (0) 207 993 4699.

.

GOWER HR TRANSFORMATION SERIES

This series of short books explores the key issues and challenges facing business leaders and HR professionals running their people management processes better. With these challenges comes the requirement of the HR function to transform, but the key question is to what and how?

The purpose of this series is to provide a blend of conceptual frameworks and practical advice based on real-life case studies. The authors have extensive experience in all elements of HR Transformation (having between them held roles as HR Directors and Senior Business Managers across a range of blue chip industries and been senior advisors in consultancies) and have consistently come up against the challenges of what is the ideal new HR model, what is the value of HR, what is the role of the HRBP and how can they be developed?

Whilst the guides all contain a mix of theories and conceptual models these are principally used to provide the books with solid frameworks. The books are pragmatic, hands-on guides that will assist readers in identifying what the business is required to do at each stage of the transformation process and what the likely options are that should be considered. The style is entertaining and real and will assist readers to think through both the role of the business and transformation project team members.

SERIES EDITOR

Ian Hunter is a founding partner of Orion Partners, a consultancy specialising in providing independent advice to organizations considering outsourcing their Human Resources department. He has worked for a number of leading management consultancies, including Accenture and AT Kearney and has been an HR Director in two blue chip organizations.